Figurative Keys:

MW00937025

This is a work of non[...]
organizations, and ev[...]
either are used fictitiously for purposes of
entertainment. Any resemblance to actual persons,
living or dead is purely coincidental.

© 2019 Tia Deas Norfolk, VA

LaTia &
Cigi,
Thank you so much
for your support! May your
business continue to prosper! And come
out on top! Please read & enjoy! And stay
in touch!

Tia Deas

Figurative Keys Series

Figurative Keys to Locked Doors

Figurative Keys to Toxic Cycles

Figurative Keys: A Guide to Overcoming

Coming Soon

Figurative Keys to Family Matters

Daily Figurative Keys

Dedication

I dedicate this book to broken pieces of me that were made whole when I decided to take accountability of my pain and use it to process me.

This book allowed me to overcome.

Tia Deas

Acknowledgements

First and foremost, God, you are everything and I thank you for the opportunity to praise your name out loud. He is the heart of every matter.

I have an extraordinary family that supports me from near and far. I thank my fathers and my mother for all they do and have instilled in me. I thank my son, Tristan, for being awesome and keeping me going. I thank my little brother and my big sister for loving me in spite of myself. My godfamily literally keeps me going when I feel like giving up. Thank you, Mrs. Nikki and your family for taking me in and caring for me and my child like we are your own. And the family near and far, you are beyond appreciated for always supporting me and guiding me in the best possible way.

My friends are beyond extraordinary. Every time I thought I was ready to go ghost and scream out in anger because things were getting tough, they were there. I could not have gotten to this point of clarity without you. You know who you are. Thank you. Seriously.

I'm supported by friends and family, but strangers have taken over my heart. The people who support me just because, thank you. The people who took a chance and bought the books in the past and this book, because they see a black woman trying to change the world. Thank you. You are appreciated.

To the four single mothers that exposed themselves in this book, I cannot and will not stop thanking you enough for being vulnerable with me and an audience. You are powerful beyond measure and I am grateful just to know you.

Everyone, before you read, know that I thank you from the bottom of my heart.

Please enjoy!

Thank you for your purchase. Please read and enjoy

Connect with Tia

Email: figurativekeys@gmail.com

Twitter: @figurativekeys

IG: @figurative_keys

Facebook: Figurative Keys

Website: Figurativekeys.com

Tia Deas

Here's to Overcoming

Chapters

11. Stop being afraid of let go of people.
12. Give yourself peace, stop searching for it in everyone but you.

13. Discuss, don't fuss.

As usual, I like to take a different approach to the growth I want to come.

After reading the chapter titles that we are going to dive into, please take a minute or two to brace yourself to deal with yourself. Sound crazy, right? But I am serious. Dealing with ourselves is ONE of the hardest aspects of life that we constantly avoid. Talking about our problems instead of covering them up is another one. But fixing, fixing our problems. Man, oh man, we do not like to endure pain within the process to progress. But this right here is an opportunity to grow and glow. This is an opportunity to extinguish and exonerate items in your life that keep holding you back. This is the opportunity to master everything you face in life, including single motherhood.

Please indulge carefully.

A few questions before we start.

Why do you think having tenacity is important?

What does mastering your fate mean to you?

Can you see yourself growing if you are not willing
to change?

You know how people used to get to me? They would mention someone stated I talked about them or they would mention someone talking about me in a negative light. I would try to act like it didn't phase me but it boiled me up inside because I often wouldn't understand the angle, the honesty, or the energy of the people involved speaking on my name.

That was the most frustrating thing to me. What do you gain from talking about me? What do you manifest in your personal life that helps you from speaking bad on me or continuing to perpetuate a lie about me, something they know isn't true?

It would literally irritate my soul that I cared so much about people talking about me in a bad light. It affected me so much that I began to shift my personal feelings about myself into negative adjectives and assertions that I felt encompassed how I was viewed.

The issue was that the problem was not within me; it was simply around me but because I didn't protect my energy, my space, my heart; I allowed inadequate people to lessen how I felt about myself and ultimately how I moved in life.

Always wanting not to step on anyone's toes or be viewed in a negative light because I was over sensitive to how others viewed me, my intentions of being honest and upfront were often misconstrued. I became a robot to fit into a box of no drama and no character nor personality because I didn't want to offend anyone. It worked for a while. No one had any negative things to say until my light started shining again.

Then and only did the rumors start flowing and the gossip got louder in my own ear on things I know I never did and on people I know I never been with or even spoken to. So even in doing what everyone deemed right in moral character and staying in my lane and space, I offended someone and they decided to try to dim my light.

However, this time around knowing myself and where I'm ultimately trying to be mentally emotionally and spiritually I didn't allow what I knew wasn't true to affect me.

You can believe what you want about me.

You can talk to whom you please about me.

But what I won't do is allow your opinion of me to shift how I move.

You don't have much power or that much courage to be the master of my fate.

I am who I am.

I am Tia LaBree and this is Figurative Keys: A Guide to Overcoming.

You can and will.

Figurative Keys: A Guide to Overcoming

Chapter 1: Don't you dare beg for anyone to stay.

Chapter 1: Don't you dare beg for anyone to stay

I've done it a time or two myself. So yes, I got the right to talk about this shit. Oh you thought this was a love letter?! It's not. So fix your attitude and fix your face because I've become quite assertive in speaking my own peace even if it offends you. If it does, I understand, but don't cope by shutting me out and not facing the reality that not everyone will not agree with your way of thinking. Don't let your reactions to a situation you can't control allow you to miss out on the blessings associated with struggle and growth.

I've lived carefully for the longest wanting and needing public and private approval of who I am and what I do. It becomes tiring though having to constantly acknowledge everyone's opinion and straddle that line of what is right and wrong in everyone's eyes but my own.

Me, I'm most important. Me. Say it with me. I am important. I am the most important person in my life. Outside of God and your child or children, that is. But seriously that self-love is a hard task to tackle because it has everything to do with you and nothing to do with anyone else.

We naturally like to bond or be surrounded by love and welcoming faces sometimes so much we would ask not once, not twice, but maybe even three times for someone to stay when they want to leave.

We might not beg but we go through the motions of nobody can treat you like me. Nobody will do you better than I will. If you leave, don't come back. Sound familiar? Now I got your attention, I guess. Begging isn't baby please, baby please anymore; it's more of bet she or he can't do it like me.

It's staying in a toxic situationship because you rather have someone to tear you down and apart instead of you being alone at night. It's allowing someone to degrade the authenticity of who you are and what you deserve because you rather not be regarded as single or lonely. It's contemplating self-hatred based on your incapacity to make someone else happy instead of inflicting self-love upon yourself by YOURSELF for yourself and be alone. It's disregarding the standards of a healthy relationship for the bare minimum of a title or purpose in another's life that doesn't consider you worth respecting instead of coping with yourself.

Don't think I don't feel the sting of my own words as I'm typing them out now. It's settlement because you are afraid to allow someone that isn't entitled to your love to stay because you don't think you can love yourself the right way. But if you can't do it right, still don't allow another to do you wrong. Life lesson I'm learning day by day. I rather learn how to cope alone than put up with insufficient activity that inadequately burdens my ability to love and trust another person.

Do we settle naturally because we see the potential that someone possesses? Yes, but realistically their potential doesn't protect the reality of your feelings and your heart. You still realistically have to deal with their incompetence when it comes to you. But the thing is, about all this, you don't have to. You don't have to ask anyone to stay. You actually can open the door for them to leave.

Why, because learning how to regard yourself highly enough to stop asking people to stay leaves you first in line in your own life. And that's step number one to overcoming hardship.

Death in Companion(ships)

A little part of me died
When I let go of the fact that no one stays
Yet you're still here and all in the way
Of my condition to prosper despite the odds
When people leave and say goodbye
My tears no longer fall and I don't crawl to any
doors to beg for more of what I know I can give to
myself
The lack of love that I feel is real because they
could've stayed but if they did, you wouldn't have
come my way and made me fall into this love
withdrawal that is based on the physical and mental
aspect of not giving up
Yes, this girl is tough and tenacity is what I have in
my heart to stay together and not fall apart when
you finally reach your goal or purpose and tell me
that you always knew that I would be better off
without you.
A little part of me died.
When I let go of the fact that everyone leaves
Yet; you came back around and still give me what
you think I need: companionship.

And I let you stay.

Reflection Time

If you have read any of my books in my past, you know I am very adamant about self –reflecting and taking the time to look at your actions so you can make accurate changes. Some things in life take time though and will not possibly happen in a day. On these reflection pages that follow each chapter reading and/or poem, I want you to acknowledge what has been happening that you know you need to change or how you plan to improve going forward. Do not beat nor batter yourself up in this moment. Just talk yourself through what you are about to overcome. Write it out; that's the first step to making a plan become reality.

Tia Deas

Chapter 2: Start talking back to the storm.

Chapter 2: Start talking back to the storm.

I told the storm. To pass. I said storm you can't last. Go away. I command you to ... I know y'all know that song. And some of y'all when y'all hear it even feel the words in your soul. So when and why did we stop talking back to the storm?

Think on it. Don't answer all at once. This title caught your attention. Why? Was it a personal feeling that said I have stopped talking back to the storm? Was it guilt like maybe I could've been a little stronger and wiser in that last situation? Why oh why have we stopped talking back to the storms of life?

I know personally I felt like my storms had too much power and longevity that my stamina couldn't maintain. I figured remaining silent and still in God's peace would keep me together and move the storms out the way. But when the rain didn't leave and the thunder got louder, I guess I got mad. My prayers then became disclaimers of if I can't get this, can I at least get that and if this last too much longer, I'm going to stop caring. As if God took my sense of humor to heart, I would laugh until I cried about my predicaments. Didn't make the situation better but at least I was smiling.

But then I started to look back over the lessons and blessings that came from previous storms. I realized the storm wasn't happening to me. It was happening for me and I was going to outlast anything it gave me. But I had to start talking back to it first.

It wanted to give me strength yet here I was letting it take away my power. It wanted to give me endurance yet here I was thinking I lacked stamina. I couldn't understand why the storms kept coming until I realized I was still going. Hope that one didn't go over your head. Read it again. I couldn't understand why the storms kept coming until I realized I was still going.

Man. The same lesson kept appearing and I'm too busy trying to shield myself from the rain that I forgot God was an umbrella. The same promises he gave before exist now and I was too beat down and battered to understand that my tongue was the weapon holding me back because I felt it was all I could hold onto.

These storms aren't meant to break you nor take you to a place of defeat. They are set in place to help you articulate the things you know are intended for your life. We are to be fruitful plentiful and blessed because we come from the most High and this is what he said to us.

So now that we understand our tongue is our weapon and God is the umbrella, our vernacular should be a little different, a little stronger, a little bolder. When the storm comes and tries to drown you, the lyrics that say you can't drown me, my God surrounds me should start to make a little more sense. Or when the thunder is louder than the voices around you, you understand the lyrics when they state when my God speaks, you have no choice in the matter, you have to cease.

Basically you have the power to push past any storm and even talk back to it when you understand it never had the power in the first place, you did. And you always will. Next time you feel the storm coming your way and the rain starts to beat a little harder on your windowpane, clear your throat. Next time the thunder and lightning try to take over your night, clear your voice passageway. And tell the storm what it is you think you need to.

I usually like to start out with oh you're back for more? You just like defeat don't you? You realize I just get better with time?

But my stamina, my endurance, my power it's too much for the storms that come my way. I talked back so much the storms have stopped coming for a while. But I'll be ready for whatever when they decide to come back.

All I'm saying is life will always give you storms in different forms. People from your past, losing your job, losing a loved one, failing at things you're superb in or at. But when you have the tenacity to tell the storm it can't and won't win, it tends to go away because the storm can't handle a person that talks back.

Storms are designed for the weakened and disabled. People who don't know how to articulate what's for them will be for them. The ability to overcome is always spotlighting what you have and never what you lack. Something about the weapon of a tongue that has tenacity to know it'll always win. I'm telling you try talking back to your storm.

Bet you, it won't snap back.

Full of It

But can I talk to you about the trifling men that
stumble into our life half-drunk off the wine that
they sip to make them forget they had problems
before you and they have nothing to do with you.
Those personal attitude swings and raging angry
moments don't mean a thing to me because I'm
where I need to be and you can't take me from a
good place because this ain't the race to hell where I
refuse to dwell with all the negative energy from the
enemy that you're trying to put into me so I'll
digress.
But can I talk to you about the trifling men that
stumble into our life half-drunk off the wine that
they sip to make them forget they have problems
that occurred before you and you will never be a
trash can to dump into.
I keep having to tell them I'm full. So they can take
themselves and their baggage to another place or
another face that's willing to take on problems that
aren't hers and let him mess up her world.
Won't be me anymore.

Reflection

Another opportunity to look at the chapter lesson and/or skill and figure out how to use it to your advantage to overcome hardship going forward. You got this!

Chapter 3: You have to be a balance beam.

Chapter 3: You have to be a balance beam.

You will never be healed if you continue to blame other people for the way you are. It must be accountability for how you let the hurt of other people haunt you.

But balance? Man did I wish I had that shit when I text my ex asking to talk about the past. Or even when I text my ex best friend about the fact I miss her in my life and I wish we could work it out. Or when I let that man I hate walk back in my life and fuck it up with his words of hate spewing because he saw I was happy.

I wish I could have balanced out my feelings with the actions that would come. I am a single mother of the most vibrant six year old boy that is a balance of all my ball of emotions and the balanced mindset of his godfamily. I wish I could take all the calm of strangers and spew it on my life at times. I wish I could and would be in control of my feelings when life throws its little curve balls my way trying to trip me up.

I have the tendency to fall and get back up mad because I knew I could have avoided the trip. Play on words. Hey, I like them. Sometimes my laughter and my sarcasm keep me smiling when life tries to throw a foot out that I can't jump over with my own strength. But that's just it. I'm not utter destruction. I'm not a mess. I'm not a failure. I am a balance of learning to be myself and feel in moments so minutes later, I'm still okay with the person I am.

I've learned that allowing myself to forgive myself first balances out my hate and distaste for those that attempt to take what happiness I've decide to surround myself with bring. I'm still learning how to not wallow in the downs because things will always start to look up. I'm still learning that no matter how bad it gets with people and things, it can always get better.

So how did I cope with the bad so it doesn't outweigh the good? I've literally learned to become a balance beam. I'm a whole lot of emotion capped out in one human so I've decided to be a little bit more logical so my feelings have a tad bit of common sense attached to them. I've decided how I feel doesn't always outweigh what I know. I've decided what I know will not always match what I feel. But I've also come to the conclusion that it's okay to feel how I feel in a moment and STILL do the right logical thing that will lead to the best outcome.

With no balance, one side starts to outweigh the other and when things get confusing, you blame yourself completely for what you didn't use in the moment.

If I make an emotional decision, my mind says you should've been smarter than that. If I only use my logic in a situation and it turns out bad, I say to myself you should've attempted to care and not be heartless. But when I combine both my logical with my emotional to make a decision on how to move forward, there is no guilt. There is no wondering if I should've could've would've done anything differently. I stand solid in my decision and deal accordingly with what follows.

Not everything in life will turn out right or how we want it to. Having the ability to understand that when you do what's best for yourself in your eyes, you eliminate the regret that comes when things don't turn out for the best.

Being a balance beam comes with understanding that you have to take the good with the bad. Being a balance beam comes with understanding you have to feel after being hurt and you have to think through all your problems anyways. Being a balance beam allows you to overcome struggles because you know you did right by yourself and everything will eventually fall into place anyways.

Stamina

I'm still trying to convince myself it's okay for
letting you treat me that way
I'm still trying to forgive myself for giving you
access to feelings you didn't protect
I'm still trying to maneuver out my feelings because
your dealings definitely left a mark
I'm still trying to move silently away from the pain
and not play the blame game when it comes to you
I'm still trying to rewrite my own story so it won't
be a boring tale of boy meets girl
I'm still trying to manage under pressure that I'm
26 and single but hesitant to mingle because of you
I'm still picking up pieces of my life and trying to
fit them back into place
I'm still trying and I think that's the best part of
you, not me.
You taught me to still try.
Thank you in advance.

Reflection

An opportunity to look at the chapter lesson and/or skill and figure out how to use it to your advantage to overcome hardship going forward. You got this!

Chapter 4: Don't you dare belittle your shine to let them glow.

Chapter 4: Don't you dare belittle your shine to let them glow.

Does the way you operate offend someone around you? Have they told you to act a little less like you and a little more like them? Have you been asked to chill out? On multiple occasions? Of course, hopefully you weren't doing the most. But y'all get my drift.

Sometimes your light is bright. When you enter the room, no matter what is going on, you become the center of attention. Why? Because, you are it. And you know this. Nobody like you. At all. And so honestly speaking, sometimes, people around you who can't handle your light or glow want you to dim your light so they receive what they think they are entitled to.

This is a book about overcoming right? So what do you think I'm about to tell you to do? If you guessed, be yourself ANYWAYS, you're right. It's way too many opportunities in this lifetime for you to grow and glow. Allowing others to stop that chance because of their personal indifferences is what I would say is BEYONDDDDD me!

Confidence is a trait a vast amount of people lack, but need in order to allow their gift to grow to its potential. People will come into your life simply to take you away from your purpose because they wish they could have it. They want what you have so discouraging you from doing it for any reason makes them think they are better. But in all honesty, most people who have a problem with your shine hide their distaste. They instead smile in your face and encourage you daily hoping and praying you fail. They won't tell you their intentions and they won't even show signs of disapproval.

But pay attention when you get awards and when you get recognition, because the people who aren't readily and really in your corner show face then. I've been a self-published author for a year now. Of course I had support when I told people I was publishing a book. Had hundreds of retweets and shares and only sold 29 books that first week. Oh, but it gets better.

A close friend of mine at the time said to me those IG likes won't carry you into success if you're not willing to change how people look at the single black female. He was right but I didn't feel like I had to change the world just to get people to read my book. Yet, his advice in that moment showed me he was actually rooting for my success and was not trying to take from me, but give to me his perspective so I could succeed. Now that is a good example of illumination.

Let's talk about dimming this light though. Had a good girlfriend, we went back some years. She would pop up every now and then as friends do and it would be like we talked every day. She actually bought the book too. The second day of the presale.

Fast forward to me being endorsed by a celebrity. God blesses people like me when deserving. She text me and said how did you manage that? Shouldn't be selling your soul to get likes and fame. I didn't see a Lol and no laughing emoji so I guess she was serious. She must've realized I was taken aback by the comment so she continues I've seen too many people like you get a lil fame and change. You're regular, don't let these endorsements and people knowing you make you think you're more than you are.

Tuh. Crazy part about it is I read it a few times before digesting it. I thought on it and about it actually considering she could be right. But nahhhh, shawty was hating because I had a gift she didn't possess.

It's a difference between shining light on an issue to illuminate a person and blinding the eyes of a star because you don't want to see the truth. It's crazy though because I knew her for more than 10 years and I knew I could take her to the top with me.

Tia Deas

Because my top has nothing to do with celebrity endorsements or fame. My top is impact and people changing their lives because they decided to grow with me. But she couldn't see what really illuminated me.

Your character will either shut you out or take you a long way. My tenacity to overcome is only because I choose to not let the naysayers get in my way. Just because people don't understand your blessings or your glow, doesn't allow them to shut your dreams down or take your gift from you.

If anything I hope you understand that your gifts from God can never be dimmed by man. You will only overcome defeat in the mind when you take the time to see the thing that illuminates you also brighten what helps me.

It's never a competition of who can shine the best. It's a battle of how bright can we be together if we include each other and forget the mess...

Fake Love KNOW Light

Crazy how the ones that do you wrong play victim to a system of you were the one that hurt me instead of taking accountability and responsibility for the actions they took
But look
As maturity creeps in, we have to learn to preserve our energy and good intentions for those that actually have the ability to listen
With concern and discernment on how to grow themselves in health and wealth not focusing on the weaknesses and deceiving options around us to cheat ourselves out of struggle.
As peace settles in, we have to learn how to let go of displaced hate and unnerving blame for people that have nothing to gain or lose from the interactions we choose to take with them because they never had anything to give to us anyways but hey.
Crazy how the ones that do you wrong play victim to a system that they didn't do wrong and you didn't do right.
This is honestly how people who can't shine try to dim your light.

Reflection

Simply the opportunity to look at the chapter lesson and/or skill and figure out how to use it to your advantage to overcome hardship going forward. You got this!

Why I'm Mastering Single Motherhood: Heiress Darby

Single motherhood is what you make it, just like everything else in this life. The most known phrase about motherhood is "hard work" but is it really? Being a single mom can be overwhelming and stressful at times only when I focus on the negatives. When I look down at my mini me, all positive energies emerge. My stress turns into peace, my tears into laughter, and my hurt into healing, which makes it all worthwhile. So to me being a single mother is easy, being an adult, now that's the hard part

Take a mental break! We are done with Part One!

What Have I Learned Thus Far?

Chapter 5: Make your OWN perimeters.

Chapter 5: Make your OWN perimeters.

Make my perimeters? About what? That would be the question that comes to my mind when I encounter this chapter. So what are my perimeters and why are they important? I learned the hard way how easy life functions when you set your own perimeters for how you operate and how you allow others to operate with you and by you. Starting to make sense yet?

Perimeters are just the guidelines you set in place to govern what's going to happen in YOUR life. If someone steps outside the perimeters, you know how to regard them and how to move forward. If someone stays true to the boundaries that you set from the jump, you understand there is a mutual respect for what you are establishing and where y'all are attempting to go on this ship. Friendship, relationship, etc. whatever it might be, it's a ship and the goal is to make it to a new destination. You can't make it from Point A to Point B without any guidelines on how things should go and be. It would be like having a crew of people on a ship with no map and no true direction except the wind that carries the ship when it blows hard enough.

The maps that we use in life even have keys that explicate what all the symbols mean in the illustrations. Stay with me now. If the map that shows us how to get from Point A to Point B has symbols that are explained in a key, they have perimeters to what can be interpreted through their illustrations or guidelines on what you're supposed to be able to see. So if a map can guide you in direction based off a key that explains how and why you view the illustrations the way you do, why can't you provide instructions to those that come into your life on how to operate when it comes to you.

Why can't you be your own tour guide to explicate how to navigate through your life so you don't end up off track with someone who can't even read the guide or understand the key? Why are we so willing to let people who don't live like us or even more or less know us come in and do whatever they please with our time and space?

Y'all know why I'm so mad writing this chapter though? Because I do it oh so often unconsciously.

I get comfortable with people and let them decide who and how they're going to be with me because I don't want to lose their companionship or the benefits that come with having them in my life. I let them talk to me any kind of way. I let them decide the perimeters of when they're going to deal with me. Because I'm so stuck on what guidelines they have or the perimeters they set that I forget I got my own.

You are the captain of your ship. You are the master of your fate. You are the one making the key for other people to read and decipher what you desire to do. You explicate yourself so others can allow them to either adjust or abort the trip because their travel method and your key or guide doesn't match up.

You can avoid destruction or lots of time and travels if you know where you're going to go and if it's going to be worth it. Prime example being, I wanted to talk to this man I had known for a long time. He was a man of good character in my eyes. He was respectful and very articulate.

Yet, his guide or his key also let me know upfront he wanted nights of intimacy and days of silence meaning he was only good for me and to me in the night but I need not try to establish friendship or companionship outside of the sheets. He set up his guide meaning he gave me the key to understanding the only destination we would get and go to upfront: the bed.

That's not what I wanted though. Not saying I wasn't physically attracted to him because I was, but I'm past the part of my life where I believe sex is going to keep me near when there is no other connection.

Stimulate my mind, hold a conversation, show me your respect doesn't only exist when my legs are open or my mouth is available to you. Whew.

Lemme get back to the topic. My point my key didn't match up with his. His guide on what he wanted or needed from me didn't align with my own perimeters of where I see myself going or what I wanted or needed from that particular ship.

Remember ships take us places. Well we wanted two different destinations. We had different keys. We had different guides and we definitely had different methods to accomplishing where we were trying to go.

My point is honest and transparent: figure yourself out so your key and map don't change up based on who is trying to make a trip.

Make your own perimeters. And don't allow those who don't fit into your guide to change up your key.

Reflect on this chapter!

What have I learned?

What can I utilize?

Is there anything I need to change?

What resonated with me personally?

Chapter 6: Stop letting the weather control your temperature.

Chapter 6: Stop letting the weather control your temperature.

Whew. It's getting kinda cold outside. Chilly, nippy, whatever you want to call it. So are you going to be affected?

Will you begin to act cold because of the outside factors that surround you? Basically are you your environment? Or summertime heat when that time comes. Will you let people come in and heat you up with petty arguments and grumbled disapprovals? Will you let them make you turn your AC off and burn up with them in the heat?

The question at hand is who controls the temperature in your body? Is it the weather outside of you? Or in simpler terms, the people surrounding you and their actions. Or do you regulate your own temperature because you don't like people messing with or turning up your thermostat?

Think on it before you answer so quickly. When you get to the point of realizing your own sanity and peace is more important than other people's expectations and perceptions, you will not get hot. Nor will you stay cold. Because you control your temperature.

Lemme say again for the people who didn't want to face the reality of that statement the first time: When you get to the point of realizing your own sanity and peace is more important than other people's expectations and perceptions, you will not get hot. Nor will you stay cold.

Let it sink in. SLOWLY. Don't miss the blessing in this lesson trying to speed through it because it actually applies to you.

Now let's talk about it. What other people do and how other people act you cannot control. So why let what you can't control, also known as the weather, make you feel some type of way, aka your temperature?

Yes it was a play on words from the beginning. I speak in riddles. I apologize in advance.

But seriously, how other people get down around you shouldn't affect how you move. Be set in your own expectations and your own ways so theirs doesn't have the capacity or tenacity to bother you at all. The concept of only being responsible for self applies in this moment. Having yourself in control eliminates others being able to realistically change how you're feeling.

That's just touching the surface though. Let's get a little more in depth. The heart is a muscle. It functions based off blood circulating in and out of it. When someone has the power to upset you, note your heart begins to race and your body temperature warms up. When someone disappoints you, you slowly pace out your heart speed and you turn cold both in body and mind.

How can we honestly eliminate someone from getting under our skin to change our body temperature anyways? Glad you asked. You protect your mind and body like they protect theirs. Simple and very easy. Remember the consistent thing about people is they change and function to what benefits them and where they're trying to go, whether you're going with them or not.

But you have the power and ability to also be consistent in how much you take in from people.

Don't give them access to how you regulate what you do.

Don't give them power to shake your world up in ways that might cause damage.

Simply move with purpose and don't allow those of no purpose to get in your mind, your train of thought, or your heart.

Guide your thermostat by taking people at the value they present, not the one you wish to equip them with.

Reality is a harsh thing sometimes to face, but if you do, you eliminate allowing people that are meant to be left outside the AC to burn themselves up or those people that need to freeze out your heated room of comfort and solidarity.

How do you control the temperature? By protecting your thermostat, or in better words, your heart, mind, and feelings, from people that weren't supposed to know how to turn you up or down anyways.

I would've missed the bus

If I knew you would be like all the others,
I would have left when you came.
Not literally but figuratively moved my body and
mind to a space where your ingenuine character
wouldn't have left a mark on me so every time I
wake up I think is he okay and I start my day
thinking of you instead of concentrating on me.
Losing focus of the goal I placed in my own heart to
not fall apart when a man decided to come in and
stay but when I fall short of perfect and the
imperfections start to outshine what is considered
normality for a single black female, you up and
forget the manners you first presented yourself with.
You listen to the gossip and laugh with the audience
of people who don't know a single thing about me
but wouldn't last a day or two in the shoes I fill
daily trying to make sure you actually measure up
to the man you thought you could be for me but you
lacked within yourself. And well if I knew you
would be like all the others, I wouldn't have come
at all. Now I'm in between feelings and left in
fuckboy withdrawal.

Reflect on this chapter!

What have I learned?

What can I utilize?

Is there anything I need to change?

What resonated with me personally?

Why I'm Mastering Single Motherhood: Shaqona Payne

A mother's love is unconditional ensuring that her child is always protected by any means necessary. There was a point in time when I felt alone and hurt because I could not financially afford to keep the lights on in my home. The innocent look on my daughter's face brought many tears down my eyes because I felt unworthy and ashamed that I was not able to protect my daughter. During that time, I was working late nights and many hours throughout the week to ensure that I was able to afford childcare.

Striving for the ability to afford food to eat and clothing on her back gave me every reason to fight to provide and establish a better life style for my daughter. My daughter was my breath of fresh air knowing that I have someone who solely depends on my every move. I want to be my daughter's first role model when someone ask "who do you look up to and why." People tend to think because you have a college degree that you would be successful and making plenty of money. However, being a college graduate did not make me a success; I credit that feat to my daughter, to motherhood.

Chapter 7: Stop thinking you deserve a seat at the table, earn it.

Chapter 7: Stop thinking you deserve a seat at the table, earn it.

Help me help you. That's how most business and even personal relationships formulate and grow. But don't think you are entitled to any of everyone's good vibes and positivity from the jump.

Reciprocity. I use the word oh so often to try to get the point across that you can't be out here taking what you aren't willing to give. If I have a table, and you don't, something has to be presented to me in order for me to understand why I should let you be at my table.

Oftentimes, we come empty handed and open-minded to friendships and relationships expecting the other person to understand we're lacking in something and need assistance with. But not everyone has a kind heart to give and not be able to receive. It's a few people in the world out there, more than we think but for this instance we're speaking on now, you gone have to work.

Do I mind sharing my table? No, not at all because I want us all to eat, but do I need someone who isn't trying to grow eating off of me? That'll be a negative. Not if I can help it anyways. The purpose of a ship is to take you to another place. Meaning we start one place and we should end up somewhere else. Not we stay in the middle of the sea and hope for the best. Personally, I can't swim and I rather not depend on someone who's content where they are in life to be the only one that can save me at sea.

So back to this reciprocity word that I like to use. You are not always going to be able to give other people what they give you. Not everyone in a relationship will be equally yoked. But if I'm the heart, attempt to be the mind. If I'm the pen, attempt to be the paper. Understand the tabletop cannot stand on its own. It has legs that support it and attached themselves to the bottom. Basically it has a foundation.

So now think of a table as a foundation and a starting point whenever you are meeting someone new that you wish to join. You can't just slide your chair up under someone else's foundation not knowing or understanding what's on the table or what went into making it so steady. That is why most chairs are made specific to the table and not the other way around. Not saying one is more important because you can eat standing up at a table or eat on a chair with no table, yet the two together is more beneficial than apart. They come together when they understand the purpose.

People sit in the chair to eat at the table. Or people eat at the table while sitting in the chair. Notice how the shifting of words can place more or less power in different objects. Take the time to understand the elements of the table you wish to sit at. Be sure you have a chair that compliments the table and doesn't take away from the design or technique used in foundation of the table. Honestly speaking, if the chair you wish to bring isn't adding to the table already set in place, it would be better to just build your own table and stop depending on others so you have someplace to eat. If it's not equally yoked or reciprocity or growth happening from your union of your chair with someone else's table, you're taking away from what you didn't deserve in the first place.

It's never a race of who can build their own table first and get chairs pulled up to it. It's an understanding that tables are established with time and hard work. It's a blessing that tables don't have time limits, though people do. If you're not willing to put in the hard work to build your own table so you won't have to eat off someone else's, then understand you gone have to work to figure out their foundation and it's functions meaning put in more work! You're going to have to pay mad attention to detail and take notes whenever you can. Then you're still going to have to self-evaluate your chair to figure out whether you fit at someone else's table.

But at that point, at least you would have earned it. If I were you, I would start with myself by myself making a table, or a solid foundation, for myself because I honestly don't want to have to earn the right to sit at someone else's table just to eat if I can build my own. And be actually fit and made for what is best for me.

Just never think you deserve what you didn't help build. That's always going to end up a bad deal.

Let's reflect on this chapter!

What have I learned?

What can I utilize?

Is there anything I need to change?

What resonated with me personally?

Chapter 8: Pay attention to the red flags.

Chapter 8: Pay attention to the red flags.

Whew. If I could only tell you how many times I saw the red flags and just kept on going because I said I was strong. I knew nothing could defeat me. I knew my power and my tenacity would get me through. Man, I was dumb and subject to my own stupidity of submission to toxic people and things.

It's called a red flag for a reason. Though flags often show victory or dominance, in this instance, it has a different meaning. It is one of caution, one of tread lightly, and sometimes one of avoidance. This is like the game of Monopoly. Do not enter, not do pass go and collect $200. I love that game. I used to play everyday with my dad when I lived with him. Don't worry, I'm not getting off topic. I'm bringing everything full circle. I went to live with my dad at 16. I had gotten in some trouble with my mom and this was to make me better as a person because my mom felt as though I needed help.

I did. I lacked self-awareness. I lacked pride in who I was. I lacked responsibility for my own actions. I lacked understanding. I lacked self- love.

My mom was a teacher and she was a great leader in the classroom, but nothing but action and orders at home. I always felt like I was getting the anger and frustration of the silent cries of a teacher. I never felt loved like I thought she loved her students. Don't get me wrong, I was bad. I didn't listen. I sneaked around. I stole things. But all for attention because I needed someone to pour into me what I felt was poured into those students she taught during the week. I ended up running away from home. My dad came to get me actually.

Running away was red flag number one. Some family and family friends saw it as a cry for help. Others suggested a good beating would fix everything. But the people I wanted it to affect only saw it as an opportunity to send me away. Being sent to live with my dad was honestly my red flag number two. No one knew. My dad didn't really know me. We had had conversations and we had postcard correspondence because he was military and always on the submarine. I knew he cared despite what people said. But he was new to me. He told me I had a clean slate. He meant it. He gave me an opportunity to be someone I wasn't before in a home that encompassed love and direction.

Yet, I crashed the car he gave me and fought a girl before track practice almost getting arrested. I had everything a girl could have wanted, yet I messed up. These were red flags three and four.

Before I got to red flag number five, I decided that I needed to fix myself. I know I said it lightly but that's the truth. It's always been something in me that yearned for more from others, instead of focusing on what it is I could give myself. And then when I didn't operate well with what others gave me, I never took the chance or opportunity to forgive myself. I forgot how important I was focusing on everyone else and what they could and can do for me.

Red flags are only ignored when you're focusing on other people's intentions instead of your own. I'll say that again. Red flags are only ignored when you're focusing on other people's intentions instead of your own. You are your own responsibility. Stop looking to gain reassurance from everyone else but you.

When we are clear in our intentions with ourselves, the red flags are clear and we avoid what we do not wish to engage in.

It's only when I realized I'm dope as fuck by myself because I am who I am and I'm going to do what I'm going to do did I start to see the red flags before the occurrence instead of after.

Know who you are, that's how you keep them red flags afar or even honestly out of sight.

Put on Notice

As stated in the chapter, red flags are there for caution. They are often put in life for redirection. Let us see if there are any red flags we have right in our face that we are trying to deflect because we know it is NOT a reflection of us.

When is the last time you apologized to yourself?

When is the last time you took time to forgive yourself?

When is the last time you took time for yourself?

When is the last time you forgave someone?

When is the last time you decided to deal your feelings?

When is the last time you talked calmly with an enemy?

When is the last time you checked your tone of voice when speaking to someone?

When is the last time you dealt with your own attitude?

When is the next time you are going to love yourself for you without anyone else's approval?

Break Knowledge

I'm tired of being left behind and I can't lie
I'm frustrated with the purpose of being impactful
and tactic in the way I speak
So you will know to change your ways and make
better days to come
Because you're still young in mind and time so you
can fix all the things I couldn't.
I'm tired of being undervalued in price and peace
I'm frustrated with the practice of being regulated
by standards of people that didn't have to walk in
my shoes and exist how I live but give all the
common advice to problems that they didn't deal
with it and that's just it.
I'm tired of being used and abused and picked at
from perimeters to determine angles of how you're
going to get to me or get at me because I'm finally
following my dream.
I'm frustrated with the perception that my
complexion deems me less than what I really am
and compares me to statistics and missions that are
greater than me. And though my tenacity is real and
this isn't a big deal, I'm tired.

And I know I need a break.

Reflect on this chapter!

What have I learned?

What can I utilize?

Is there anything I need to change?

What resonated with me personally?

Why I'm Mastering Single Motherhood: Jadyne St. Julien

So. News Flash. I just realized I am a Single Mother. Wow. Now I question, why it took me so long to identify myself as such.

After a very long, dragged out, and painful split between myself and my son's father in August of 2017, I am just now identifying with the title, "Single Mother". I feel the reason is because ever since the breakup, I feel MORE supported and less alone. I have a very dependable, operating, and loving support team that consist of family, co-workers, and friends since the breakup. While in that relationship, between the both of us, things got VERY distant and toxic. We both needed something from one another that was not being met and I started to see that the love I was seeking, not only was not in the relationship, but I had also lost for my own personal self. I felt the most alone during the course of the relationship than I had ever before in my life. I noticed I had become so use to settling and making sure things were good for the collective, that I sacrificed my long term happiness, starved myself spiritually and emotionally, and settled for short term smiles.

We had different love languages, belief systems, and different ways of expressing ourselves to each other. None of these things truly BREAK a relationship but when you have all of these missing and a solid foundation was never established, it was

bound to be short term. In that relationship, I had
the physical and financial support
(EVERY woman's dream, Right? WRONG)
but emotional and spiritually I was a Single Mother
in a very lonely relationship, that functioned but did
not define love for my soul. Now that I have left
that relationship, I feel like I am a Willed,
Passionate, and Supported Mother that has been set
ablaze to her purpose and goals. Finally free to put
myself first and though I still have love for my
son's father, taking steps back have revealed to me
how I needed to grow and get comfortable with
letting go of what doesn't serve my highest self and
feed my soul.

Now that we are acquainted with my journey to
realization and identification, what being a single
mother to me means utilizing ALL of your
resources.

Often people don't utilize all their resources for one
of a few reasons. One, they fear rejection and
judgment. Two, they are unaware of the resources
available. Once we have left the blind spot of
ignorance, as a "Single Mother" I feel compelled to
tell you that it is your responsibility to face EVERY
Fear in your thought pool. As a single mother, I
understand that my child is always gauging me from
his perspective.

Children calibrate with their parental/guardian
energy fairly quick and when I realized that, I knew
I had to rid myself of Fear in order to make sure that

seed did not sow itself into my Child's thought pool. The only thing to fear on this earth is Fear because it wears so many masks. For our children, we must unmask these truths and use them as stepping stones to inner-standing of ourselves.

To me, being a Single Mother also means prioritizing my peace. My peace consists of me protecting and consciously prioritizing out my time, my space, and my attention. The way I prioritize out my energy for my peace's sake depends on my emotional and physical space, in the present moment.

My needs (physically and emotionally) constantly change, day to day, moment to moment. So I put forth a lot of energy to staying present with my feelings by self-reflection, meditating, staying rested and hydrated, and giving myself safe spaces for me to hear myself think and feel. For my child, my peace of mind has to be intact and also protected and nurtured by those I tribe with. Being a single mother has taught me that if my cup is empty, I have nothing to give to my children or my tribe, and in order to keep a full cup, I have to know how I feel and what fills my cup and keeps it over-pouring.

Being a Single Mother comes with its challenges but I believe when you tap into your strengths, that is where the magic lays. I had to realize as a single mother, my dream deserved a chance to flourish and my children need to see me go through my journey;

I don't hide from my feelings, as I mentioned in my prior relationship. I own them and I inner stand that the emotions are there to guide me to my truths.

Being a single mother to me means women can literally do anything we set our mind to. Single motherhood also taught me that I am a gift to the world, not the sacrifice, and my happiness is my responsibility to create and maintain. Being a single mother taught me growth and that I am forever evolving.

Tia Deas

Take a break: We're DONE with Part Two!

What Have I Figured Out Thus Far?

Chapter 9: With energy comes everything.

Chapter 9: With energy comes everything.

You can't tell me you don't feel the energy, whether good or bad, in a room when you enter it. Or if you can't feel the energy of a situation or circumstance, you should tread quite lightly. The question that comes to mind when I say this would be are you deserving of what you're looking for or does your energy match the intensity of the situation you desire?

Crazy spin to this chapter right? But this is how I see it. If I want good man energy, I need to possess some good woman energy. I need to match the intentions or inflictions of the person that I'm seeking to have around me or beside me. What's the point in seeking good friends if you don't possess the stamina to maintain being a good friend? What's the point in seeking a soul mate or person to marry if you don't possess the stamina to maintain being a partner or person of commitment?

Can you match the energy required to the things you desire? Your energy and your disposition honestly carry a lot of weight in your relationships though it may not seem as such. We thrust our energy in praying about things that we often can't change about other people instead of thrusting energy into being what it is we want to see in the other person. As if complaining or exerting energy into a problem and dysfunction is going to fix it. Praying over it. Fussing over it. Crying about it. Venting about it. It changes NOTHING.

But if you took the time to thrust the same energy to change what you can in your own life that will affect the situation in a positive way, you might change the outcome. We oftentimes stay stuck in a moment feeling hopeless, taking what energy we do possess to fret and worry about everything that can and go wrong. We do not focus or point out energy in the positive manner of what's working and what's good so it can be a forward motion in the discrepancy.

I'll give you a personal story that I've yet to tell but a few people about. I had a boyfriend; we were on and off for years. We had one of the worst dysfunctional toxic relationships known to man but the friendship we possessed was solid. But anyways, we started out as friends.

We learned every little intricate part of each other for the friendship. We invested into each other with nights of laughter, watching movies, and telling each other how we could conquer our dreams. The intimacy was beyond the realms of physical contact because we honestly didn't have any. We placed so much energy in each other to thrive, despite what happened in and out of each other's reach, we remained strong friends.

Well, we crossed a line that we could not come back from. We decided to date each other; he asked me out and I was beyond overjoyed by the union, I forgot to keep that same energy. Whew. Hurts to write but I messed up one of the best things of my life because I could not and would not maintain the same energy within the relationship because I did not have the stamina to deal with the negative energy that surrounded us. I invested more energy in the people asking questions about our union. I invested more energy in seeing what he did wrong when it came to the opinions and speculations of other people. I have a bad habit of letting outside energy control how I operate within. And that is where I failed myself and him.

Now did he mess up in the union? Yes, but that accountability piece will fuck us up more when we don't take it. I didn't allow myself to place my energy in the good times we had anymore. I didn't allow myself to thrust my energy into fixing the problems we had between us too busy trying to thrust my energy into protecting what other people saw in us and about us. My energy then turned his energy and we both were focusing our energy on the wrong things. My energy being in the wrong place lost me the love of my life.

But it brought clarity to one thing. One thing that will never change: with your energy comes everything. What you allow to consume your energy will either be the beginning or end of what you always hoped for.

So if you want a good man or woman, put your energy into being a good woman or man and maintain that same energy once the union happens. Maintain that same energy when strife comes up in the relationship. Keep that same energy when the comfort zones start to creep in. And definitely apply stamina to the energy when struggle comes into place.

Because your energy will always either keep you going or suck you dry of what your heart desires.

Into Now

I'm tired of explaining what you can't understand
Transforming my inner workings just because of
your demands
I tell people fix yourself before you adjust to me
I'm way beyond the mental and what you happen to
peep through screens
This mental outweighs my emotional and it's all
personal
How I decide to let you in or kick you out
My feelings are often sensations of overused words
and underused cliches
Momentary coping mechanisms used to progress
through our days
My now is full of I'm better than this and I'm way
past that
Holding myself accountable to understand and
realize that
I can't change a thing about you until I change
myself
You are the epitome of my fear to conquer my own
depth
I get so tired of explaining what you have yet to
understand
Placing myself in park because I'm scared to be the
one in command.

Reflection for Readiness

What can I say I am ready for?

What am I able to say I am ready to overcome?

What has been holding me back?

Is it me or my surroundings?

Chapter 10: The reaction matters, not the mistakes.

Chapter 10: The reaction matters, not the mistakes.

I'm ready for that release stage. I'm tired of surviving and coping. It's the healing and harvesting part of my season in life. I did have opportunities to walk away from tragic situations and didn't. I grew from them and will continue to use them for my good. I don't want to keep my growth to myself though. Too many blessings and opportunities to come if I share and promote a better way of life. It's just the simple fact I know people expected me to fail, yet I'm here thriving anyways and it feels good.

Stop using your pain as your identification. My story isn't me and never will be the characteristics that can define who I am as a person. But how I react in circumstances going forward will portray my personality and honestly who I am to complete strangers.

Understand your worship can never be situational. You can't praise dance when it's good and fall out when it's bad. You can't remain still in a mistake because you made it. You can't. You won't. You wouldn't. You focus on the good that came from the blessing. There is no failure in life because everything can be utilized as a lesson. It's only when we focus on the bad that we miss out on the good.

That rhyming and rhythm sounded real good but how we move forward is based on what we are using from behind us. Yikes. So yes I'm saying you're going to have to use what was supposed to break you to build you up. I've believed and said to many and plenty of people that things don't happen to you, they happen for you. What you take from the so called mistake is the energy and education to grow and make better decisions moving forward.

But a better way to look at it would be there are no mistakes. There are blessings and lessons. Either way you learned or gained knowledge on how to react. Now comes the tricky part. How we react to situations or lessons or even blessings can turn something or someone around. Whether it's our facial expressions, our words of choice, or our adjustments from the mistake, we react and it's noticed.

Mistakes are expected. Everyone makes them as no one is perfect. But how you view them and how you adjust to what comes from them is what you must focus on. It's not about falling down; it's about how you get up. It's not about how you strike out. It's about how you readjust when you're back up at the plate to swing again. I could rant on and on about how much what you do changes people and how they view you or I could be transparent and tell my reactions or readjustments to mistakes caused me friendships and relationships, deals and dreams, etc.

I lost out on things because I was so busy fretting over the mistake that I didn't look at all at what I could have and possibly did gain to move me forward.

The goal to get forward and keep growing from the things we do. So adjust and reevaluate how you allow yourself to move forward after a mistake. Because it's not the mistake that matters, it's the reaction.

React to rejuvenate yourself. React to release positivity. React to readjust the right way so you can be the one that ends up on top.

Chapter 11: Stop being afraid to let go of people.

Chapter 11: Stop being afraid to let go of people.

Why was this one so hard? Because I have difficulty letting go of people. Honestly.

People often define your character by what you don't do for them anymore. It's a you changed or I'm not going to be cool with you anymore because you don't want to be who you used to be to me. So what! Things change. Most people don't change but the circumstances they allow themselves to be in are evaluated and then they decide to leave because they see something is unhealthy, toxic, or simply not worth their time.

But you know how people get under our skin? They slew insults and say comments that insinuate we are bad people or people of bad intentions. We then start to overthink our own actions instead of staying strong in them and try to figure out a way to change their personal opinions of how we are. But why? Who cares? We are humans and we will forever agree to disagree on topics that concern your heart or even feelings.

We have to make sure we protect our own heart and feelings instead of reflecting on the words of someone who may have never had theirs intact.

Hurt people hurt people and by that I mean when someone feels as though you are leaving them when they expected you to stay longer than the last one they let in, they make a point to try to use their words to hold you captive in something that was never meant for you anyways.

Yes the red flags are there, but we learned about those in Chapter 8. Been done, done that. Stop allowing people to get in your head and allow you to feel some kind of way because you no longer want to stay. Let go of people who serve you no good. And I don't mean put them on do not disturb for a few days and then when they say something to incite conversation or an argument, you reply fast because you want to call it closure.

That's you belittling yourself yet again to a system of mind games meant to destroy your personal willpower to deal with things that you shouldn't be doing. I'm giving you honesty. People know how to get under my skin still and I have the hardest time letting go of people especially if they got close to me and I started to care. It's practically over at that point trying to force them out my life. They'll say something and my smart ass mouth is ready to respond and tell them what it really is.

But the growth in me from writing out my own flaws and misconceptions when it comes to how I handle people has allowed me to see that if I let go (all the way go) of people in the first place, I won't have to deal with their problems that they try to place in me and on me.

But how do you let go of people? Blocking them is one way but that's a toxic trait that I had to stop doing. This is how I've learned to let go. I literally write everything out that occurred between me and the person. Everything!!! And I write what I need to forgive them for and what I need to forgive myself for. I hang it up on the wall for me to see every day until I get tired of seeing that dirty laundry or that baggage that's not worth carrying anywhere in a good relationship I might find. Because once I get tired, I'm over it. I rip it up when I'm tired enough and I move forward forgiving myself first and that person.

It doesn't take contact or closure with that person for you to push through. It's a personal thing.

Letting go of people. So stop being afraid to do it.

Sorry

This isn't even an I'm sorry or I apologize thing
Though I know the start does have a ring
I figure I would tell you about the traumas and the
dramas that got me to this place where I think you
need to know I'm with fault and I can't help but
hurt you because I'm hurting too
And though you think you can heal me and get me
in a good space, you're wrong and I know I'm right
when I say I shouldn't have ever crossed that line
and spent time with you
To develop and envelop feelings of want and need
because our souls sought out aspects that only
implemented that we were people of good character
and morality so it would work out somehow
But then I run because I'm just too scared and
you're just too sharp and the art of understanding
that just because we're good people doesn't mean
we're good for each other because I messed up and
I hurt you
So I wanted to say I'm sorry or I apologize so you
would know I feel bad but I understand that the
closed door on us was way beyond my mistakes and
your heartbreaks.
Us parting ways was to teach me how to forgive and
pray for you anyways
But I guess saying sorry or I apologize is just easier
and feels like the right thing to say.

Reflection for Reasons

What would be my reasons to overcome?

1.

2.

3.

4.

5.

6.

7.

8.

9.

10.

Let them be your motivation to keep going!

What have you learned about your own tenacity?

Chapter 12: Give yourself peace, stop searching for it in everyone but you.

Chapter 12: Give yourself peace, stop searching for it in everyone but you.

Assertiveness, motivation, and self-esteem.

Which one do you lack in and which one do you have the most? Is your self-esteem in the hands of the people surrounding you or is it an internal affair that you constantly have with yourself? Is your motivation based off the approval of the people that smile in your face and whisper behind your back? Or tactfully speaking, are you assertive about the shit you want to get done?

Are you concrete in defining your own limits on how you allow others to invade and occupy your time and space?

All these factors ultimately control your peace. I can be assertive but if I don't have a clear plan of what I wish to do, anybody and everybody can come to me with a plan and I then become their puppet to their dreams and their execution. It all seems simple in the scheme of where do I want to be and what do I want to do but it's kinda complicated, exaggerating, and irritating to have that much power over SELF.

The reason most people fail in achieving peace is because they do not believe they have their own power to achieve it. We fall victim to placing other people's perimeters of what peace is in our heads and follow their guidelines or timesheets when ultimately it doesn't have anything to do with them.

You are in control.

You have the power.

You. You. YOU.

You have to take everyone else out of the equation and figure out what need in order for you to get to a peaceful state of mind.

My peace may never be your peace. I can find peace in a chaotic room with students yelling hyperboles and allusions to the top of their lungs. This is because I find comfort in learning and growth. I find peace in knowing my presence promotes the things I desire out of life. My peace is all about constantly growing into the woman I constantly know is within me and is me.

But what is peace to you? Where do you find comfort and where do you see yourself lacking in attempting to find the peace you deserve?

I can only guide you to thinking outside of the box. I can only tell you lessons I got from blessings that I know God intended for me.

You are powerful beyond measure.

Take your peace for you, because it has nothing to do with anyone else.

Can This Be My Peace of Mind or Is This Just a Piece of Life?

I often write in riddles and rhyme because it is honestly how I talk. But I am solid in saying and mentioning that sometimes we confuse peace with piece. They are homophones, yes, but completely different meanings. Peace is something we attempt to achieve for the betterment of ourselves whereas piece can mean a whole lot of different things. *cues laughter* Just know sometimes the pieces of life we let in might be the reason we CANNOT and DO NOT achieve peace within.

When is the last time you relaxed mentally?

When is the last time you relaxed emotionally?

When is the last time you relaxed physically?

When is the last time you relaxed spiritually?

Is the person by yourself allowing you to do any of these things?

Is your child or your responsibilities preventing you from those things?

Is there any piece of your life you can let go that would add to your peace?

Are you willing to let it go?

Can you honestly say how pieces of your life benefit or subtract from your piece of mind?

Reflection with Responsibility

Simple Question: What things are you going to be responsible for going forward in order to overcome?

Chapter 13: Discuss, don't fuss.

Chapter 13: Discuss, don't fuss.

Easy to say, harder to do. We have the tendency to get frustrated when people do not listen the first time so we begin to change our tone and level of understanding because they are not doing what we want them to do. Sound familiar? Because it's true.

When people do not listen when you say it the first time nicely, we're like you want me to get or be upset don't you? Anyone ever said that in their head? I know I'm not alone. But the truth is more than half the arguments that occur in this world are 90% tone of voice and infliction and 10% indifference on the subject.

I could be saying the same thing over and over, but the way I say it and why I'm continuing to say it plays a very big part in the whole scheme of things. It's a matter of understanding there are no problems that lack solutions even if it's intangible. There will always be a way to fix something even if it's just learning to walk away, move on, or let go.

Truth is I fuss all the time and frustrate myself in spirals of madness because my students don't get it the first time, the second time, the third time. Not until someone gets hurt or something happens that affects someone other than themselves. I saw the frustration consuming myself though and not the person that I'm trying to get my point across to. Though they get irritated and they change in the moment because they see that I'm upset, the behavior continues. I entered the conversation irritated already and began fussing before I allowed myself to calm my nerves to approach the issue better in the light of trying to actually fix it.

I know you're saying why would discussion have such a huge impact on learning to overcome fate? What you allow yourself to do affects how you're going to push through. If you enter conversation allowing someone to already be under your skin on something that is not so much of an issue to them, you've already lost the fight. It's like being in the boxing ring by yourself. Why do it? If you want positive results in your life, you have to promote positivity even in the moments of frustration.

You are what you do, you are what you say, and you are how you react to anything and everything that occurs to you in life. Remember that, you are your reaction to struggle and pain. Are we able to smile through pain? Yes, but it's better to use your frustrations to learn how to communicate solutions to problems you know how to fix. It's not worth the pain.

It's worth the process to learn to discuss, how to overcome rather than fuss about the disappointments that will always try to keep you down. Your power is always in your delivery. Instead of allowing the anger to drain you and allow you to frustrate another, discuss how you will and were always a problem solver.

Worried people fuss. Warriors discuss how to keep moving forward. That's what we've been learning chapter after chapter. We've become problem solvers that fix and displace the negativity of life into realistic solutions that will constantly promote overcoming any and everything. We have overcome ourselves in the process. Well I did anyways. I hope you did. I hope you learned that only you can stop yourself from the sky. Yet the sky isn't even a limit.

You overcame the limitations that other people put on you a while back when you built your own table in Chapter 7.

You overcame letting the weather tell how your temperature in Chapter 6.

You overcame being afraid to let people go in Chapter 11.

But you overcame the biggest thing when you decided to believe in a young woman of stamina. You endorsed and read a dream of mine. You allowed yourself to trust me to be a guide to truly overcoming everything that held me down. The most vulnerable I've been with my feelings yet. And you read it through and hopefully learned some things along the way.

Thank you for allowing my dream to keep going to allow you to try. You are truly an overcomer and I'm beyond proud of you. Glad we mastered this. Always remember the God always outweighs the bad.

Here is to new beginnings of freedom, faith, and finding out what's next to OVERCOME.

Reflection Resolutions

A resolution is a solution to a problem. List the problems you currently have and a plausible resolution to assist you with navigating through it using one of the lessons within the chapters you have completed.

Problem:

Resolution:

Problem:

Resolution:

Problem:

Resolution:

What chapters held the most relevance to you?
What problems did it help you solve so you can
overcome?

Why Am I able to Overcome?

Your opportunity to shine, I want nothing but POSITIVE affirmations and attributes about yourself so you can understand and encompass your power so you WILL overcome adversity && hardship.

I am

I am

I am

I am

I am

I am

I am

I will

I will

I will

I will

I will

I will

I overcame

Therefore, I AM unbreakable!!!

Afterword.

Sometimes in the process of growing myself, I would feel defeated. I would feel as if my impact was not reaching. I would feel powerless instead of powerful. But then, as if God hears my silent cry, I would receive an email, a text, or even a review that assured me I am working with purpose and all things will come into line for me if I keep steady. Knowing the impact that readers are starting to feel keeps me going.

I always said as a young child that I wanted to write books. We say a lot of things as children that sometimes never come to fruition. It's that personal motivation to make dreams become reality that kept me in this race. Time and time again, I often had to say to myself, you got this Tia. And honestly and truly, all of you reading this book do too. Never give up because it's hard. Life is hard, and having a baby while single can be harder. But personal tenacity, integrity, and willpower, that's what the sum of this book encompasses. You can and will MASTER it. Thank you so much for your purchase, your time, and just for being you.

Tell Me What You Think!

This is the part where I ask something of you. It's great to tell a friend about the book. It's even powerful passing the book on for others to read and purchase on their own. But I need feedback. Please tell me how you felt. Please talk to me about the experience so I can better service you. My DMs are always open, but reviews for the book are needed. Please visit the website www.figurativekeys.com and leave a review on the page. Please email me at figurativekeys@gmail.com. Please go on Amazon and leave a review if you can. Please go on Goodreads and Litsy and all other venues and help me expand my reach. I also have a Medium where you can read up on my new poems and pieces. My Medium is under my name, Tia Deas. Thank you again for your support!

About the Author

Tia LaBree was born in Orangeburg, South Carolina, on July 27, 1992. She grew up in Stone Mountain, Georgia and Cocoa, Florida, before settling in Norfolk, Virginia. She is the mother to a handsome son named Tristan Deas. She received her Bachelors of Arts in English Literature in 2016 and recently graduated with her Masters of Arts in Teaching English in December of 2018. She is currently in her third year teaching 8th grade English for Chesapeake Public Schools. Tia is a member of Zeta Phi Beta Sorority Incorporated and Order of Eastern Star. Her passion is affecting her community and the world. Tia enjoys reading, traveling, and motivational speaking. She has three self-published books entitled Figurative Keys to Locked Doors, Figurative Keys to Toxic Cycles, and Figurative Keys to Single Motherhood. She has overcome domestic abuse, homelessness, and depression. She uses her self- help books as an outlet to help others.

Made in the USA
Columbia, SC
22 May 2019